CONTENTS

WHY DANCE?

Dance is great exercise, and it is fun, too. There are many different styles of dance, with something to suit everyone. Dance styles can either be done solo, with a partner or in a group.

Dancing is simply moving your body to music. Some people dance for fun, at parties or nightclubs. Some people perform dance in front of an audience or for competitions. There are many ways to dance. Classical dance includes styles such as ballet, ballroom and tango. Hip-hop and breakdancing are types of street dance. Many **genres** of music have a style of dance to go with them.

Tap is a style of dancing that produces its own music! Metal plates on the soles of the dancer's shoes produce a rhythm as the dancer moves.

TRY THIS

Dance is a fantastic way to keep fit. Most dancers are very **supple** because of all the moves they do. You can burn a lot of calories dancing, and because it is fun it doesn't seem like a tough work-out either. Try putting on some music and dancing energetically for 20 minutes in your room. It's more fun than going for a run!

Careers in dance include being a dancer or a dance teacher. Dancers perform just about anywhere there is an audience, such as on TV, in theatres, clubs and at local events. Dancers can become dance sport coaches and dance therapists. Dance thereapy helps people to express their feelings using dance. Some dancers become **choreographers**. A choreographer designs the series of movements that dancers perform.

DANCE WARM-UPS

It is important to warm up properly before any exercise. A warm-up reduces the chance of injury and improves your dance performance.

It is good to start a warm-up with gentle **rhythmic** exercise. Keep both feet on the floor. Gradually warm up your joints with knee bends or arm swings, for example. Do gentle stretches like the lunges below to stretch your hamstrings and calf muscles. Do not over stretch. The fitter you are and the more often you train, the longer your warm-up needs to be to have the same effect.

How long a warm-up takes depends on your age and fitness. A teenage student might need to take 10-15 minutes to get fully warmed up.

TRY THIS

Is your warm-up good enough? A good warm-up needs to:

- make your muscles more stretchy
- make you breathe faster and deeper
- make your heart beat faster and stronger
- increase your body temperature
- allow your nerve fibres to work well
- allow you time to focus
- increase the range of joint movement
- move blood to where it is needed

At the end of the warm-up you should feel warm, relaxed, and ready for action. Then you can gently try more difficult stretches like the one above.

Remember to cool down at the end of exercise, too. It allows the body to gradually wind down towards a resting state rather than suddenly stopping. A cool-down allows you to relax physically and mentally, and will help to prevent muscle soreness and injury.

ALL ABOUT HIP-HOP

Hip-hop is a street dance style. Hip-hop dance is often **freestyle**, which means the dance routine is made up on the spot. Hip-hop dance can keep you fit and it could be a career.

Breakdancing is a style of hip-hop. It got its name from when dancers saved their best dance moves for the break section of a song.

Breakdancing includes these four basic dances,
- **toprock** - footwork steps done standing up
- **downrock** - done with hands and feet on the floor
- **freezes** - stylish poses done on your hands
- **power moves** - complex and impressive acrobatic moves

The move when you change from toprock to downrock is called a 'drop'.

You need strength and rhythm to do great downrock.

Hip-hop dancers taking part in a dance battle competition.

TRY THIS

Hip-hop dance crews often have dance competitions against each other, called battles. Try staging one. Your DJ must use the same piece of music for each person. Make the piece of music about 30 seconds long. Competitors dance and are judged to see who is the best. You can either compete as teams or individually. Gradually get down to the final two, who battle it out for the win.

Hip-hop is a very energetic form of dancing. It allows its dancers the freedom to add in their own personalities. Hip-hop dance steps require skill and experience to perfect. Hip-hop dancers practise a lot to master the basic steps and movements. Dancers with a good sense of rhythm find it easier to learn hip-hop steps.

Do the Wave

Waving is a hip-hop dance style made up of movements that make it look like a wave is going through a dancer's body.

To do a body wave, imagine an electric current is hitting the tips of your fingers. Then the current travels down your body to your feet. Start a body wave by holding both arms out in front of you. Bend each part of your arm up and down starting with your knuckles. Move the wave down your body by sticking out and then pulling in your chest, and rolling your body all the way down to your heels.

To do an arm wave, hold your left arm out to the side, parallel with the floor.

Now drop your hand down and lift your arm slightly at the wrist. Bend your elbow.

Drop your arm down. With your shoulders down, lift your chest as though taking in a really big breath.

Lift your right shoulder with a kind of jerky popping movement.

Roll the wave down through your right arm so it hangs down limply.

Collapse your chest, pulling it right in and curving your back out. Lift up your lower arm with a jerk.

TRY THIS

Try doing the whole thing backwards, as though the electric shock was coming through your feet this time. Put them together into one move.

The Resurrection

The resurrection is a street dance move, but it is done in hip-hop dance, too. The move should look almost like a video playing backwards.

This move looks great. If you get it right you can look like something from a zombie film! Make your movements smooth as if your limbs are slowly coming back to life.

Lie on the floor with your hands under your shoulders. Make sure your palms are face down so you can push yourself up.

Raise your body off the ground using your arms. Rest on one knee with the other leg in the air.

Push yourself backwards with your arms. Lean some of your weight on your knee, ready to push off.

As you push backwards, push off with your knee and raise the other leg into the air to create a rocking motion.

Rock back up onto your feet and lean back. Use the rocking motion to start to lift yourself up.

Gradually lift your body up until you are standing.

BALLET BASICS

Ballet teaches you grace, self discipline and self confidence. If your dream is to become a ballet dancer, you must practise a lot. Many of the poses are quite difficult.

Ballet dancing is physical. It takes a lot of effort to make something look effortless! A male ballet dancer will usually lift over 1,361 kg of ballerinas during a performance. Experienced ballerinas dance on the tips of their toes using special shoes. This takes years to learn. Most steps and poses in ballet have French names because the first ballet schools were in France.

TRY THIS

Probably the most well known exercise in ballet is a plié, pronounced plee-YAY. A demi-plié is a small knee bend (right) while a grand-plié is lower, with the heels coming up off the floor. 'Demi' means half in French, and 'grand' means big.

Foot Positions

There are five basic foot positions. Every basic move in ballet begins and ends in one of the five positions.

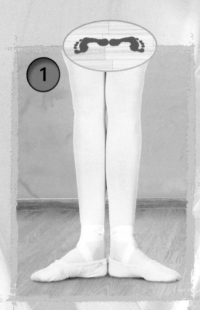

First position
The feet touch at the heels, making as straight a line as possible.

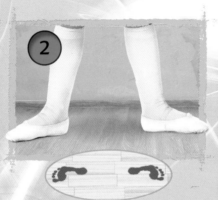

Second position
From first position, move your feet around 30 cm apart.

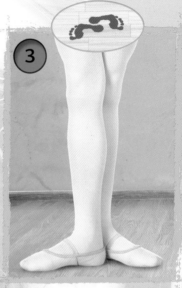

Third position
Place one foot in front of the other, with the heel of the front foot near the arch of the rear foot.

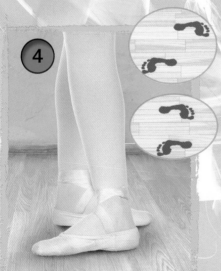

Fourth position
There are two types of fouth position, open (top) and closed. The picture is of closed fourth. For open fourth, align your heels.

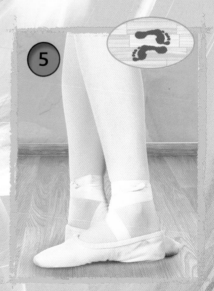

Fifth position
The heel of one foot should touch the toe of the other foot.

Arm Positions

Correct arm positions are crucial in ballet. They help balance the dancer and make the moves look graceful.

Every ballet step uses one of the five basic feet positions and five basic arm positions. The names and the positions are a little different in different ballet methods. The positions used here are the French method, which is a very fluid and elegant style. The arms are never held straight but are always gently curved.

1

First position
Hold both arms low in front of your body, with the hands almost touching. Round the arms, slightly bending your elbows. Raise the arms so that your fingers are in line with your navel.

The positions of the arms and legs and the tilt of the head give each pose its character.

Second position
From first position raise your arms to the side. Keep your arms slightly rounded. Lower your elbows and wrists. Keep your shoulders down, your neck long and your chin up.

Third position
If your left foot is in front, your right arm should be raised. Raise your right arm over your head, slightly forward. Your left arm moves to the side in line with your navel.

Fourth position
There are two fourth positions: low (above) and high (left). To do a low fourth, bring your left arm forward, slightly rounded at chest height. Your right arm is to the side, slightly rounded, palm forward. For a high fourth lift your right arm over your head and slightly forward.

Fifth position
From first position, raise the arms over the head, elbows slightly bent. You should be able to see your hands without moving your head. Your hands should be about 15 cm apart, palms inward.

INTRODUCING JAZZ

Jazz dance has its roots in Caribbean dance. The dance form developed alongside jazz music. Jazz dance isn't just danced to jazz music though. Many jazz dance moves are used in music videos.

Jazz has become one of the most popular dance styles in recent years. This is mainly due to its popularity on television shows, films, music videos and adverts. People enjoy watching jazz dancers, as the dancing is fun and energetic.

In a jazz class, dancers are encouraged to add their own personality to make each step unique and fun. Jazz steps include turns, leaps, jazz hands, kicks, sideways shuffling, rolled shoulders and turned knees.

You can jazz dance alone or with a partner.

One of the simplest jazz moves to learn is jazz hands. This is when a performer extends their hands with palms toward the audience. To do a basic jazz hands position, open your hands with palms facing forwards, and the fingers splayed while shaking your hands and moving your fingers. The arms are often straight, with the fingers spread wide open. This move is used frequently in jazz dance, using one or two hands.

A dancer doing jazz hands

TRY THIS

A jazz walk is a low walk where the knees are bent. The dancer walks by placing the toe, then the ball of the foot and then the heel down, similar to how a cat walks. Move your shoulders as you walk. Try bending one arm so it is curved forwards and the other arm is curved backwards, then swap around.

Cross Tap Kick

The cross tap kick is a great jazz move. It uses expressive hands and large movements.

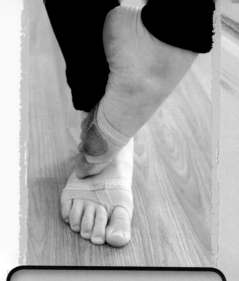

Make sure you have done a proper warm-up session before trying this move. The high kick could pull a muscle if you are not properly warmed up. Remember to smile, too.

These foot thongs help your feet to slide along the floor. They also protect the ball of your foot. Some people wear flexible jazz shoes instead.

Hold your elbows up and out to your side. Hold your hands with the palms facing inwards. Bend both knees with your left leg crossed over behind your right leg.

With your arms in the same position, bring your left leg out to the side. All of your weight should be on your right leg.

20

Cross your left leg in front
and lean forwards. Lift up
both forearms as shown.

Lift your right leg, and start
to open out your arms.

Outstretch your arms
and kick up and out
with your right leg.

TRY THIS

Try the same move
in reverse, so your
other leg ends up
doing the kick.

TRY TAP

Tap dance uses the sound of the dancer's tap shoes hitting the floor as a **percussion** instrument. Tap dancing came from a mix of ballet, jazz and clog dancing.

There are two major types of tap dance: rhythm and Broadway. Broadway tap focuses more on the dance. It is often performed in musical theatre. Rhythm tap uses mostly footwork and little arm or body movement. Tap can be done with no music at all. In Irish dancing, the tap dancers create a rhythm by using different steps at the same time. The steps are normally kept simple. The group of dancers must work together to create the sound, keeping their steps at the correct speed to match each other.

A performance of Irish dancing by the *Lord of the Dance* group.

Tap dancing can be a great spectacle.

TRY THIS

Some tap steps make one sound and some make two. Here are a couple of easy ones. A brush makes one sound. To do a brush, stand on one leg. Moving from the hip, strike the ball of the other foot on the floor in a sweeping motion. You can sweep either forwards or backwards. A shuffle makes two sounds. It is a combination of a forward brush, a backward brush, and a step, all with the same foot.

Tap uses **syncopation**. Syncopation is when the weak part of a beat is accented. If music is in 4/4 time, you can count '1, 2, 3, 4' along with the rhythm of the music. Syncopation stresses the spaces in between. So if you counted '1 and 2 and 3 and 4', the 'and' is the weak part of the beat, and where syncopation happens. Syncopation is widely used in genres, such as jazz and reggae.

Learn a Tap Move

This move is called a shuffle ball change shuffle hop step! The great thing about the name is it tells you what order to do the different moves in.

This move combines the shuffle you have just learned with some more tap steps to make a simple routine. Here's what they mean. A ball change is two steps: one with each foot where the first step does not hold your full weight. A hop is a hop on one foot. A step is a small stamp. Give them a try!

Swing one leg forwards and hit the ball of your foot on the floor.

Bring the same foot back and hit with the ball of the foot again.

TAP

Place the ball of the same foot on the floor with your body weight on your back foot.

Shift your body weight to your front foot. Then repeat the shuffle from steps 1 and 2.

Hop on your left leg.

Gently place your right foot back next to your left foot.

CONTEMPORARY

Contemporary dance is an intense form of dance. It uses elements from many other styles. It often uses unpredictable changes in rhythm, speed and direction.

Contemporary dance was developed as a reaction against the rigid techniques of ballet. The dance style can appear disordered, but it still relies on technique. Contemporary dancers have less set movements than ballet. Dancers will often take a ballet movement and alter it to work for them in their style.

Contemporary dancers performing a dance show.

There are four main techniques used in contemporary dance. Cunningham, Graham and Limon are styles named after their inventors. Release is a style named because of its breathing and releasing techniques. Cunningham is very graceful and natural. Graham concentrates on floorwork and is very grounded. Limon uses the feeling of weight and energy in the body and concentrates on breathing. Release is a great relaxation technique as well as a dance style. It uses breathing to create easy movement.

TRY THIS
Design your own dance

In contemporary dance there aren't any set moves. When deciding on a routine, dancers avoid the strictness of other dance styles. They take moves from other styles, such as ballet, jazz and hip-hop and change them. That way dancers have a completely unique and original piece of **choreography** that they can call their own.

The Fish Roll

Many contemporary dance moves are done on the ground. This one is called the fish roll! It takes a bit of practice.

TRY THIS

You could try just doing steps 1-3 to start with and rolling back to a sitting position.

The fish roll can be difficult as you can roll over quite hard onto the floor if you get it wrong. This girl is very good at them and is happy to do them on a hard surface. Make sure you practise on a soft mat instead of a hard floor!

Sit on the floor or mat. Make sure that you are not wearing anything that could stick into you as you roll, such as a metal hair clip.

Lean back and push yourself gently with one hand into the roll. Tuck your head in so you have a rounded surface to roll over on.

Roll onto your right shoulder, pushing yourself up with the left hand. Kick your legs up high. Bring your right leg down towards the floor.

Turn your face as you roll so your right cheek is on the floor. Place your right foot on the floor to break your fall as you roll over.

Gracefully lower yourself to the floor. This can be the hard bit; you don't want to belly flop! Use your **core** muscles and your left arm to control your movement.

You have finished your roll. You could push up on your arms to raise your head and shoulders at the end, too.

GLOSSARY

choreographers People who devise and arrange dance movements

choreography The art of arranging dances, especially for ballet

core The deep muscles in the torso

expressive Conveying thought or feeling

freestyle A dance style where dancers are not restricted to a certain way of dancing

genres Types or categories of dance or music style

percussion A musical instrument, such as a drum, cymbal or maraca, sounded by striking or shaking

rhythmic Relating to or having rhythm

supple Able to bend or twist with ease

syncopation Accenting the off-beat in music to vary the rhythm

FOR MORE INFORMATION

Books

Heneghan, Judith, *Mad About: Dance* (Wayland, 2016)

Storey, Rita, *Street Dance: Behind the Scenes with Urban Experts* (Franklin Watts, 2017)

Websites

BBC Get Inspired: How to get into Dance
www.bbc.co.uk/sport/get-inspired/28969977
Gives information and advice about getting into dance.

Dance Spirit
www.dancespirit.com
An American magazine website that gives dance news, fashion and competition advice for young dancers.

Love to Know, Dance
dance.lovetoknow.com
This website has history, biographies and instruction for many different dance styles.

INDEX